The Cat and the Dog

The Cast

Dog

Cat

Girls: Long ago, the cat and the dog were good friends.

Boys: They were happy until one day the cat said...

Cat: I've finished sweeping.

Dog: And I've finished the dishes. Let's eat now.

2

Cat: What's in the cupboard?

Dog: Some bread and a bit of mouse. That's all there is.

Cat: I wish we had ham.

Dog: Mmmm! Ham would be lovely. Let's buy some with our money.

4

Cat: Good. Come on, Dog. We'll go to the shop.

Dog: Off we go, then.

Both: Ham, ham, beautiful ham. Off we go to buy beautiful ham.

THE
PICTURE
FRAMER

BARBER

Today

7

Dog: Here's the shop. Just look at that ham.

Cat: Ooo-oo-oo! It looks yummy! I can't wait.

Both: Ham, ham, beautiful ham. Home we go with our beautiful ham.

8

9

Cat: Yummy, oh, yummy, ham! Let me carry it now.

Dog: Here you are, Cat.

Cat: Ham, ham, beautiful ham. I can't wait to eat my beautiful ham.

Dog: Hey, Cat. You said *my* ham. It's *our* ham.

Cat: Sorry, but it's *my* ham. I've got it, and I'm going to eat it.

Dog: But, Cat, it's *our* ham. Come down right now.

13

Cat: Sorry, Dog. It's all gone. But you can have the bone. Here! Catch!

Dog: I'll catch you one day, Cat. Just see if I don't. And I'm not going to let you live with me now. So there!

Girls: Now dogs and cats are not friends.

Boys: And dogs eat bones and chase cats.

Everyone: And cats run up trees to get away.